LITTLE WOMEN the musical

The Broadway Company of Little Women — The Musical, Photo Credit: © 2004 Paul Kolnik

Original Broadway Cast Recording available on Ghostlight Records www.ghostlightrecords.com

Cover Art: FRAVER/EMG

Piano/Vocal arrangements by Jason Howland and John Nicholas

Cherry Lane Music Company
Director of Publications/Project Editor: Mark Phillips

ISBN 1-57560-829-4

Visit our website at www.cherrylane.com

Sutton Foster © 2004 Joan Marcus

Megan McGinnis, Sutton Foster, Jenny Powers, Amy McAlexander © 2004 Joan Marcus

Jenny Powers, Jim Weitzer © 2004 Paul Kolnik

(Clockwise from lower left): Megan McGinnis, Amy McAlexander, Jenny Powers, Maureen McGovern, Sutton Foster © 2004 Paul Kolnik

Maureen McGovern © 2004 Paul Kolnik

Sutton Foster, Janet Carroll © 2004 Joan Marcus

Sutton Foster © 2004 Joan Marcus

Sutton Foster © 2004 Joan Marcus

Sutton Foster, John Hickok © 2004 Joan Marcus

Jenny Powers, Sutton Foster, Megan McGinnis, Amy McAlexander © 2004 Paul Kolnik

CONTENTS

Little Women – The Musical: Synopsis

Act One

As *Little Women* opens, we see Jo March enacting her OPERATIC TRAGEDY for Professor Bhaer, her neighbor in Mrs. Kirk's New York boarding house. Her "blood and guts" saga is clearly not to his taste. He suggests she is capable of more refined writing. After he leaves, Jo ponders whether her writing was BETTER years before, back home in Concord, Massachusetts.

Jo reminisces on those days, and we venture back to the March family attic of two years previous. Jo is rehearsing her siblings in her new Christmas play. Each sister is trying to find something to be happy about that Christmas; it is difficult with their father away at war and no money for gifts or a Christmas tree. Jo promises they will no longer want for anything once she is a successful writer, and they will all realize OUR FINEST DREAMS. As Jo runs off to fulfill one of those dreams, Marmee comes home with a letter from their father and reflects on how her life is HERE ALONE.

To help support the family, Jo has taken up helping Aunt March. Aunt March worries that Jo is not the lady she needs to be to take her place in proper society. Jo wants to tell Aunt March what she thinks of society, but Aunt March offers to bring Jo with her to Europe…if she can change her ways. COULD YOU?, she asks.

"I could change if I wanted to," replies Jo.

Time passes, and older sister Meg has one of her dreams realized: she and Jo are invited to a Valentine's ball! While younger sister Beth is happy for them, the youngest, Amy, is jealous. Meg worries about what to say to potential suitors. I'D BE DELIGHTED is what Marmee suggests. When the glamorous evening arrives, Amy tries to go in Jo's place, as she feels she's more entitled. When Marmee won't allow her, Amy pouts and acts out to show her unhappiness.

At the ball, Jo is startled by the appearance of her neighbor, Laurie, who is accompanied by his tutor, Mr. Brooke. Meg is soon smitten by Mr. Brooke, and they leave to dance. Laurie professes his need for friends, and soon he asks Jo to TAKE A CHANCE ON ME. His good nature wins over Jo, and she agrees to take that chance!

Back home after the ball, Amy and Jo have a little confrontation: It seems Amy's jealousy has gotten the best of her. Marmee tries to intervene, scolds Amy for her actions, and explains to Jo that Amy is still very much a child.

Jo is still getting over the sting of her tiff with Amy as she starts to express her feelings through her writing. Time passes, and we find Laurie inviting Jo to a skating race. Beth offers her skates to Amy, as Amy has outgrown her pair.

Intent on staying inside, Beth sits at the piano, out of tune as it is. Mr. Laurence, looking for his grandson, comes upon her musical attempts. She soon softens his hard heart and they find themselves playing a duet OFF TO MASSACHUSETTS. He leaves, but not before inviting Beth to come play his (in-tune) grand piano next door.

When Amy and Laurie come in from skating, we learn that Laurie rescued Amy when she fell through the ice! Having faced this life or death situation, Jo and Amy resolve their differences, and Jo swears in Laurie as an honorary member of the March family, officially making them FIVE FOREVER.

Time passes, and Marmee is making plans to go to Washington to tend to her ill husband—but she is short on funds. Jo saves the day, coming up with money to pay her fare. Marmee is just barely gone when Aunt March and Jo have a heated exchange, and Aunt March rescinds her offer of a trip to Europe. Instead, Aunt March focuses her attention on Amy to turn her into the model society lady she wished Jo could have been.

Before Jo can settle matters, Mr. Brooke

comes in to announce his enlistment in the Union army and to ask for Meg's hand in marriage so that he could be MORE THAN I AM. All of this seems very sudden to Jo, who questions Meg's loyalty to the family; after all, they had sworn to remain together forever. Jo's world is starting to change significantly!

A few weeks later, visiting Jo in her attic, Laurie arrives with news and a declaration. The news: With Mr. Brooke at war, he is headed off to college in Boston. The declaration: He's in love with Jo!

All this is too much for Jo. She refuses his advances, sends him off, and questions her future. Will she be able to find her way, without her sisters or her best friend? She vows her life will be ASTONISHING, no matter what!

Act Two

Back in New York, 1866: The war has ended, and Mrs. Kirk and Professor Bhaer are holding a telegram for Jo. Jo, however, bursting in, has her own news to share. She has sold her first story to THE WEEKLY VOLCANO PRESS! Soon all are privy to the news—she has sold her OPERATIC TRAGEDY, encountered earlier, only now it's better, thanks to the Professor's advice!

Once Jo comes down to earth, Mrs. Kirk remembers the telegram: Beth is gravely ill. Jo packs to leave New York immediately. She hastily makes her goodbyes.

Back in Concord, Mr. Laurence has his own plan to make Beth well: He moves his piano into the March home. Beth and her family are overwhelmed by his generosity, and soon all join in another rendition of OFF TO MASSACHUSETTS.

After the song, Jo sends a note to Professor Bhaer, telling him of her plans to take Beth and Marmee to Cape Cod with her earnings. She asks him what's new in New York. He tries over and over but just can't quite find the way to tell her HOW I AM.

Once on the Cape, Jo splurges her meager earnings on her mother and sister. All put up a brave front concerning Beth's health, but Jo and Beth privately admit to one another SOME THINGS ARE MEANT TO BE.

Back in Concord: Eventually Amy and Aunt March return from Europe. Much has changed. Meg is now a mother, Jo is now a published writer, and Beth has passed on. Things are different for Amy, too: She is engaged to Laurie, who had consoled her in Europe when Beth died. Together they break the news to Jo; after all, it was THE MOST AMAZING THING.

Later, in her attic, Jo asks Marmee how she has been able to handle the loss of Beth. Simply, Marmee insists Beth will always be with them and that Jo, too, will find she has DAYS OF PLENTY.

Jo takes in what her mother has said and finally sees how she can go on . . . and how she can keep Beth's memory alive. Jo begins work on what is to become her greatest achievement: *Little Women*, the novel. THE FIRE WITHIN ME fills her attic…and her heart…as she brings her family to life on paper.

The day of Amy and Laurie's wedding arrives. Amidst the last minute details, Jo and Aunt March finally resolve their issues. Aunt March will leave Jo her house, with the suggestion that she open a school. Her generosity touches Jo in ways she never expected.

Suddenly, in the flurry of wedding excitement, a confused Professor Bhaer enters, looking for Jo. He apologizes for arriving on such an auspicious day, but he comes with good news and a declaration of his own. First, Jo's manuscript has been bought! Jo March is a novelist! As for his declaration…

Well, he bought a kite!

But from this point, he proceeds to pour his heart out to Jo and tells her how he's finally ready to share his SMALL UMBRELLA IN THE RAIN.

Jo, always skeptical, questions their chances. Theirs would be a new kind of relationship for a new world. Could it possibly work?

That question is answered nightly at *Little Women – The Musical!*

An Operatic Tragedy

Lyrics by
Mindi Dickstein

Music by
Jason Howland

Moderately fast, restless

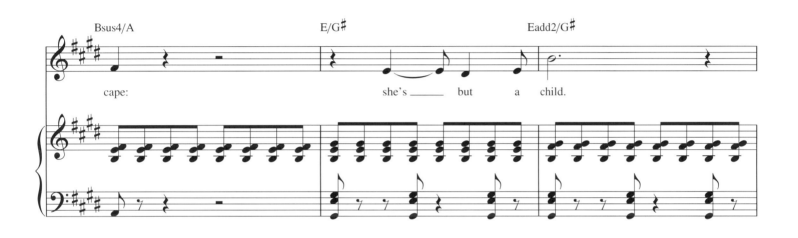

Your bit - ter - est foe! You stole what was right - ly mine ten long years a - go! You left me cold, a - lone, and for - got - ten; now I'm back to set - tle the score!

Better

Lyrics by
Mindi Dickstein

Music by
Jason Howland

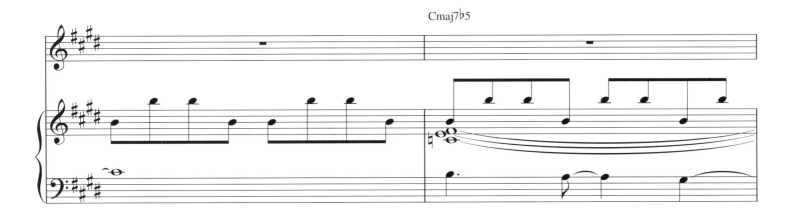

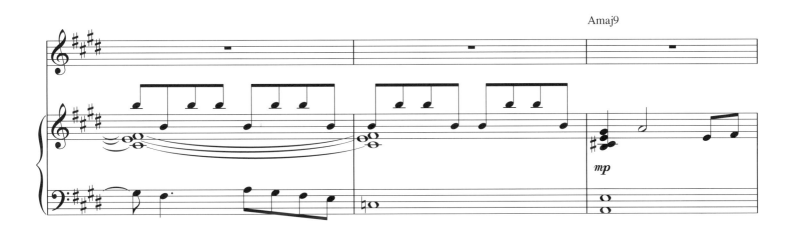

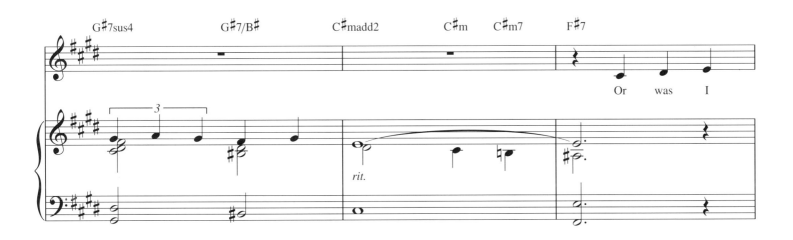

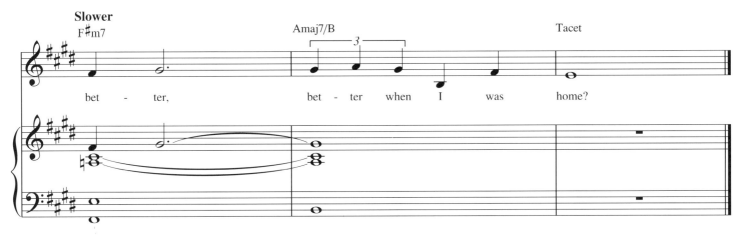

Our Finest Dreams

Lyrics by
Mindi Dickstein

Music by
Jason Howland

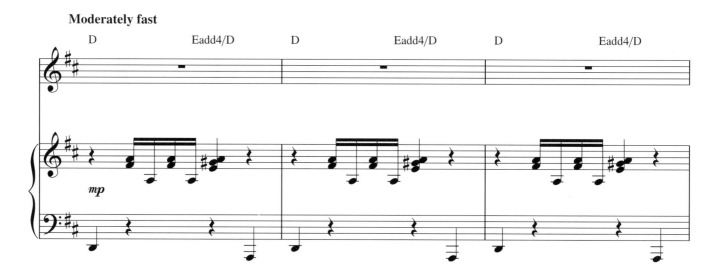

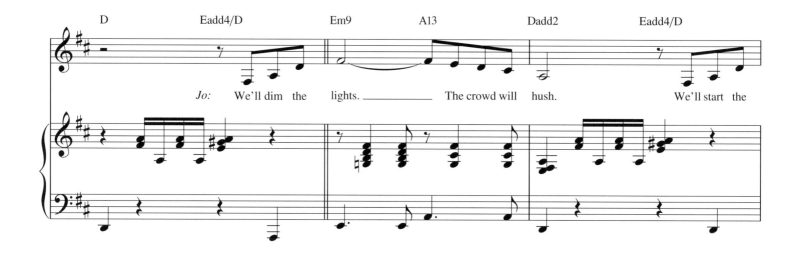

Jo: We'll dim the lights. _____ The crowd will hush. We'll start the

o - ver-ture and Beth will sure-ly blush. And when Cla - ris - sa starts to

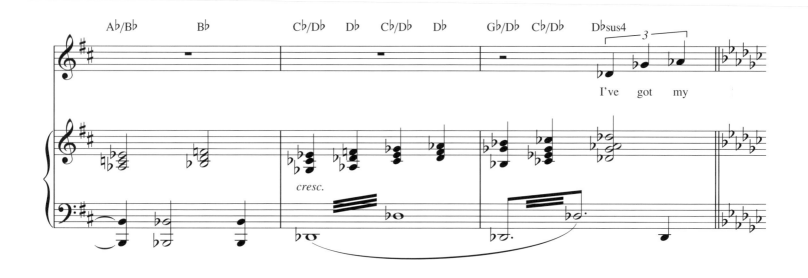

I've got my

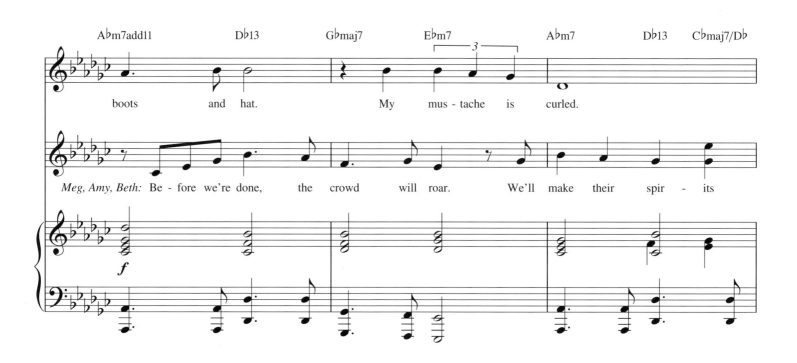

boots and hat. My mus-tache is curled.

Meg, Amy, Beth: Be - fore we're done, the crowd will roar. We'll make their spir - its

I'm mak - ing my en - trance now with cur - tains un -

soar! Our suc - cess is guar - an - teed!

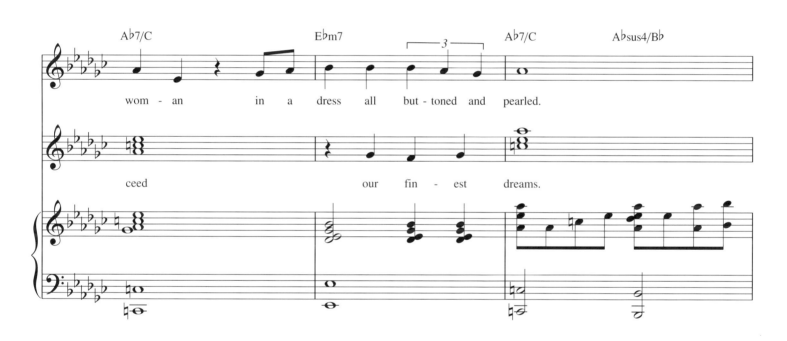

Here Alone

Lyrics by
Mindi Dickstein

Music by
Jason Howland

or rais - ing lit - tle wom - en _____ when I am here a - lone. _____ Count - ing days, _____ pray - ing for news. Is this the life

Could You

Lyrics by
Mindi Dickstein

Music by
Jason Howland

Moderately fast, in 2

Aunt March: You could nev - er bend your will. You could

prac - tice self - con - trol? Could you

nev - er fol - low through. You could nev - er bite your

pos - si - bly be shy? Could you wear a cor - set

tongue, though your tongue may split in two. If you

tight in the heat of mid Ju - ly? These are

38

I'd Be Delighted

Lyrics by
Mindi Dickstein

Music by
Jason Howland

Slowly, freely

Moderately fast

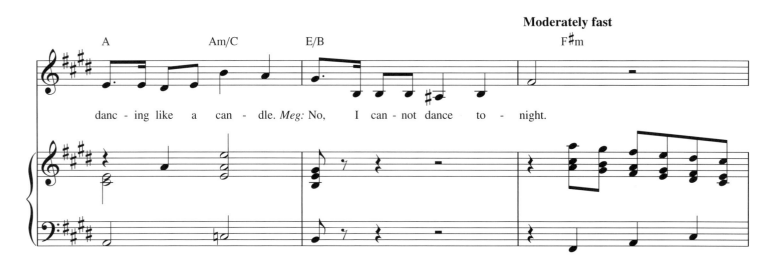

like me when I'm there? *All:* I can see you danc - ing all night!

Take a Chance on Me

Lyrics by
Mindi Dickstein

Music by
Jason Howland

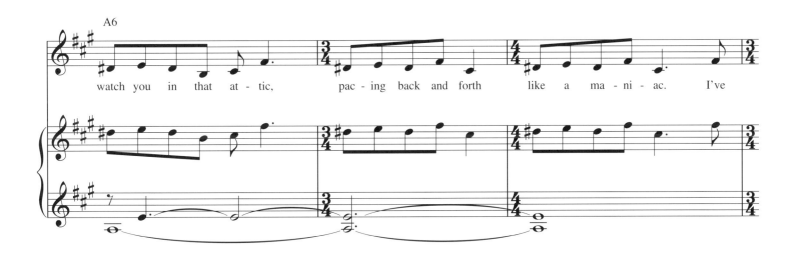

Books are sol - i - tar - y. But I see you ev - 'ry day, ____ how you live in your ___ own way, ___ and you make me want ___ to dare _____ to take _____ a chance ___ on you. ___

Eadd2
F♯add4/E
Instrumental...
F♯madd4/E
Eadd2
D/G
A/B
Eadd2
F♯add4/E
F♯madd4/E
C♯7sus4

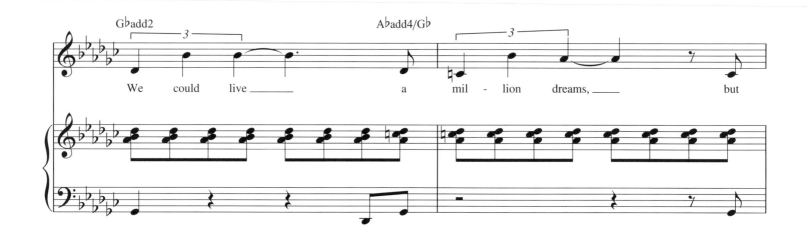

We could live _____ a mil - lion dreams, _____ but

on - ly if we dare. We could go _____ to

such ex - tremes. ___ There's so much we could share. We'll

cir - cle the world do - ing all we've ev - er dreamed of. _____ And we'll

Off to Massachusetts

Lyrics by
Mindi Dickstein

Music by
Jason Howland

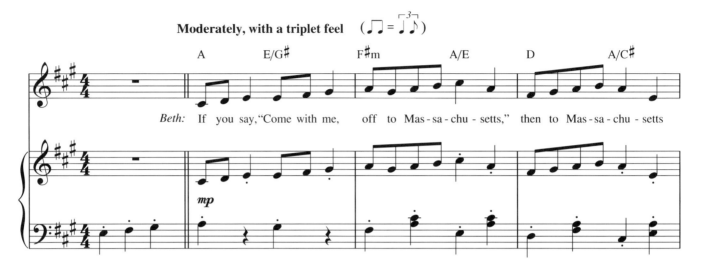

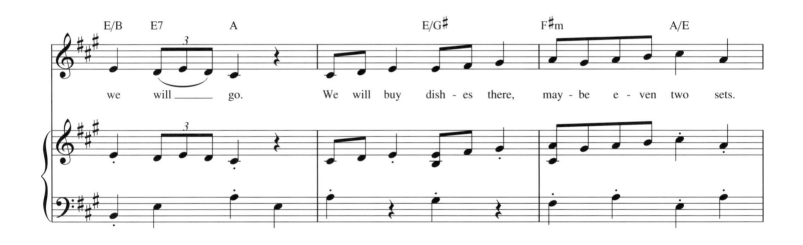

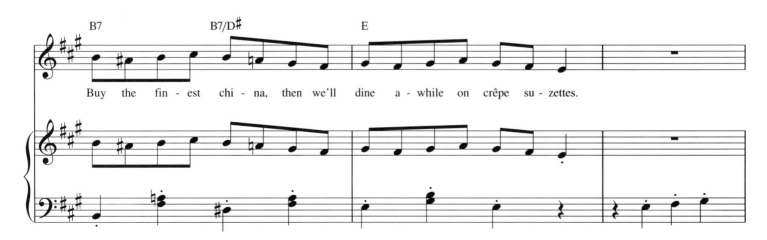

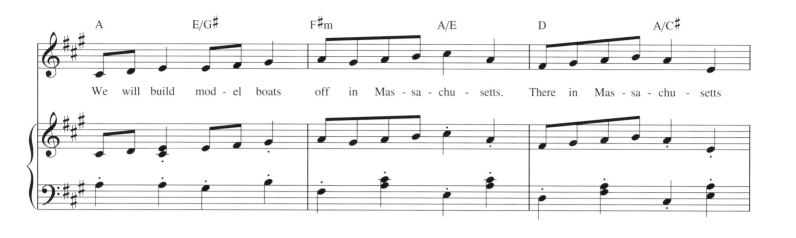

We will build mod - el boats off in Mas - sa - chu - setts. There in Mas - sa - chu - setts

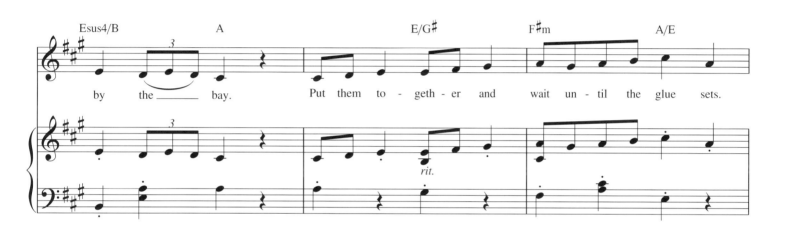

by the _____ bay. Put them to - geth - er and wait un - til the glue sets.

rit.

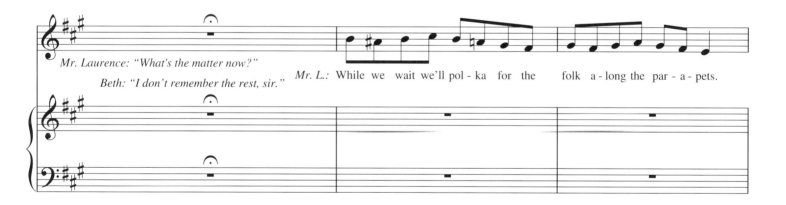

Mr. Laurence: "What's the matter now?"

Beth: "I don't remember the rest, sir." *Mr. L.:* While we wait we'll pol - ka for the folk a - long the par - a - pets.

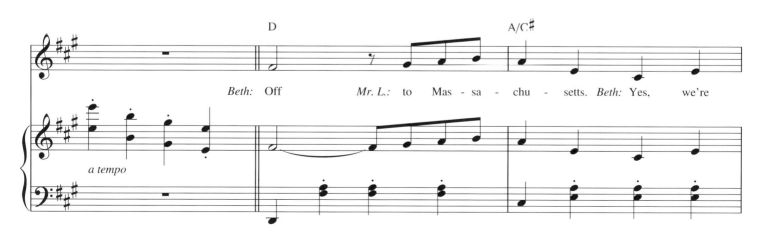

Beth: Off *Mr. L.:* to Mas - sa - chu - setts. *Beth:* Yes, we're

a tempo

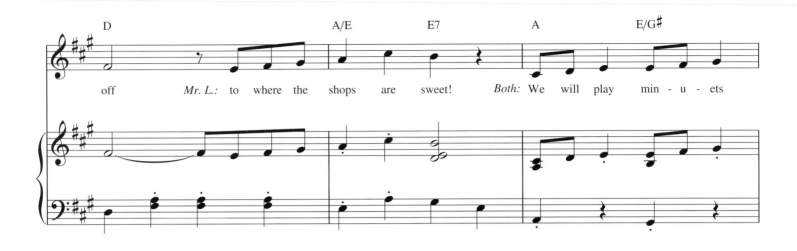

off *Mr. L.:* to where the shops are sweet! *Both:* We will play min - u - ets

off in Mas - sa - chu - setts. Bos - ton, Mas - sa - chu - setts, Bea - con Street.

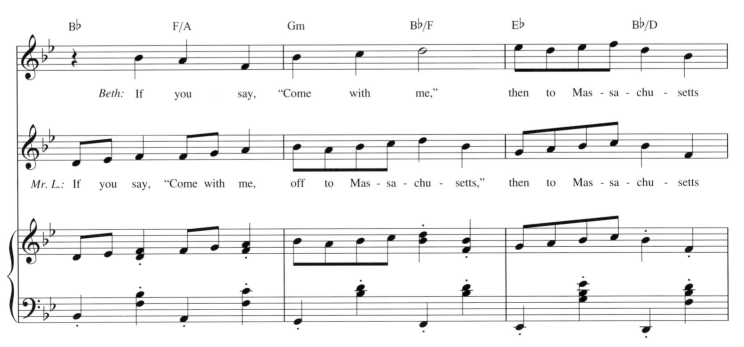

Beth: If you say, "Come with me," then to Mas - sa - chu - setts

Mr. L.: If you say, "Come with me, off to Mas - sa - chu - setts," then to Mas - sa - chu - setts

chu - setts. Yes, we're off _____ to where the shops are sweet.

chu - setts. Yes, we're off to where the shops are sweet.

We will have no re - grets off in Mas - sa - chu - setts.

We will have no re - grets off in Mas - sa - chu - setts. Bos - ton, Mas - sa - chu - setts, we,

Bos - ton, Mas - sa - chu - setts, we, Bos - ton Mas - sa - chu - setts, we re - peat!

Bos - ton, Mas - sa - chu - setts, we re - peat!

Five Forever

Lyrics by
Mindi Dickstein

Music by
Jason Howland

Meg, Beth, Amy, Jo: From this day on, we swear that we shall not be part-ed. From this day on, no mat-ter what, we're five for all for life. We'll con-quer ev-'ry foe Jo: with our broth-er by our side. Meg: And if John Brooke were

(Spoken:)

More Than I Am

Lyrics by
Mindi Dickstein

Music by
Jason Howland

Astonishing

Lyrics by
Mindi Dickstein

Music by
Jason Howland

How I Am

Lyrics by
Mindi Dickstein

Music by
Jason Howland

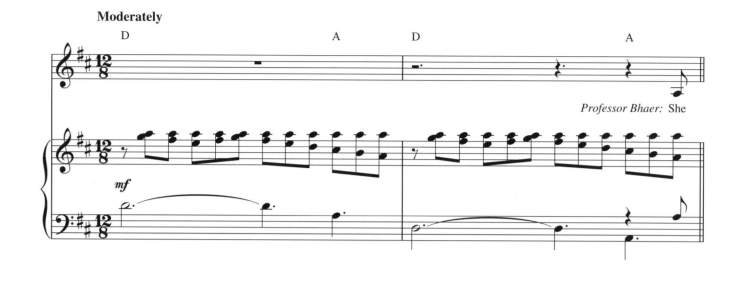

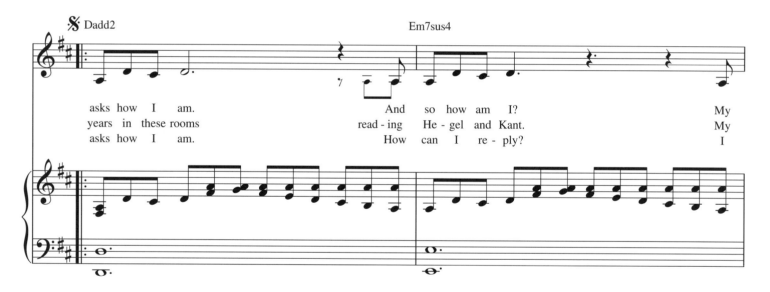

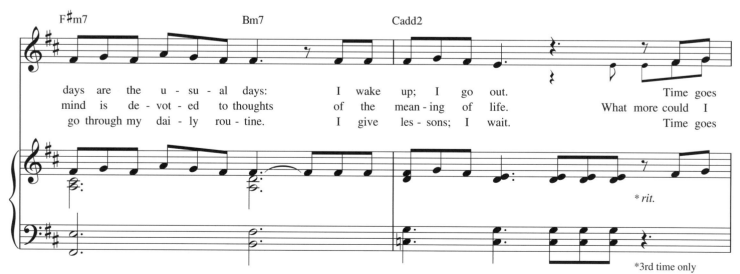

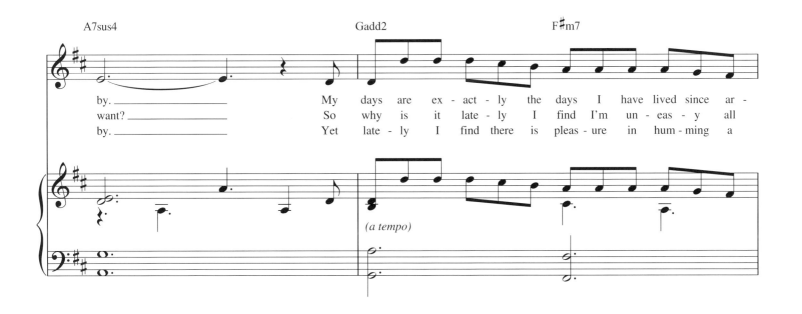

by. _____ My days are ex - act - ly the days I have lived since ar -
want? _____ So why is it late - ly I find I'm un - eas - y all
by. _____ Yet late - ly I find there is pleas - ure in hum - ming a

(a tempo)

riv - ing here. ___ In fact, how I am is a - mazed how this com - forts me
through the night? ___ And why e - ven now does my skin feel ex - plo - sive as
sil - ly tune. ___ And some days I go to the park and I sit there all

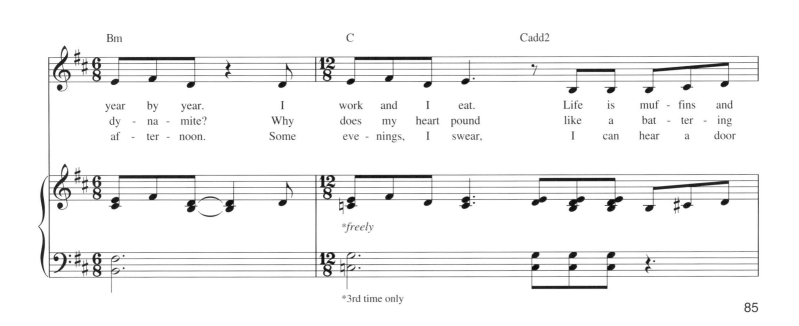

year by year. I work and I eat. Life is muf - fins and
dy - na - mite? Why does my heart pound like a bat - ter - ing
af - ter - noon. Some eve - nings, I swear, I can hear a door

*freely

*3rd time only

jam. / ram? / slam.

The house is nice and qui - et now. / How can she ask me how I am? / The house is far too qui - et now.

That is how I am.

Five

How I am is

fine!

clang and the beat of our tur-bu-lent street? Quite of-ten I think of our days in New

York.   Though, of course, since you went I have been quite con-

tent.   Ach!   I

wake in the morn-ing and all that I hear is the ab-sence of sound.

words, if I spoke, that would stick in my throat! Who asked her to change how I live, how I think, how I am? _____

D.S. al Coda

She

Coda

That is how I am.

Some Things Are Meant to Be

Lyrics by
Mindi Dickstein

Music by
Jason Howland

94

The Most Amazing Thing

Lyrics by
Mindi Dickstein

Music by
Jason Howland

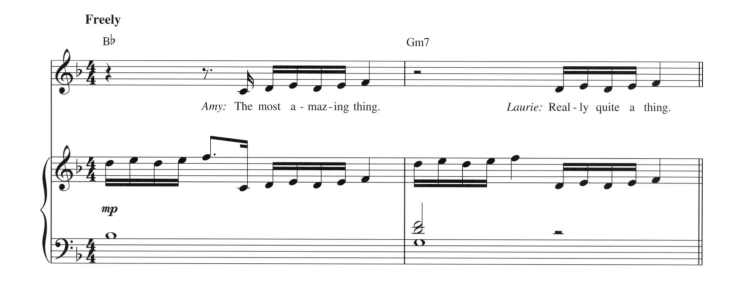

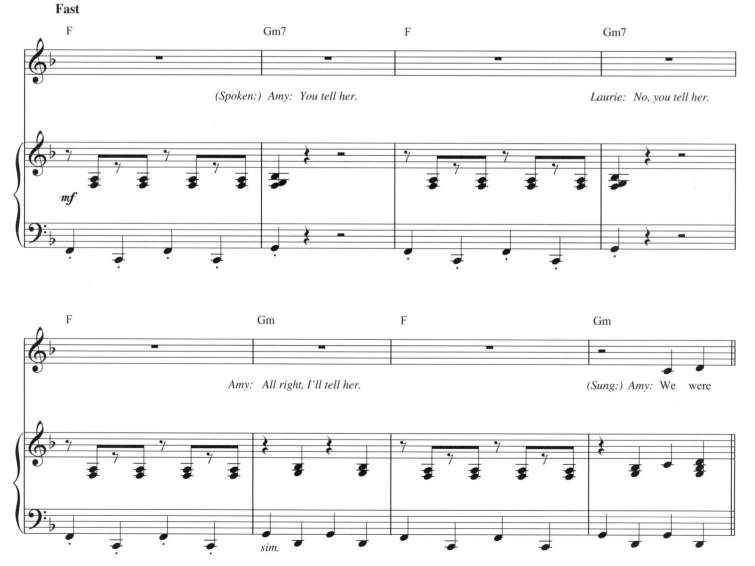

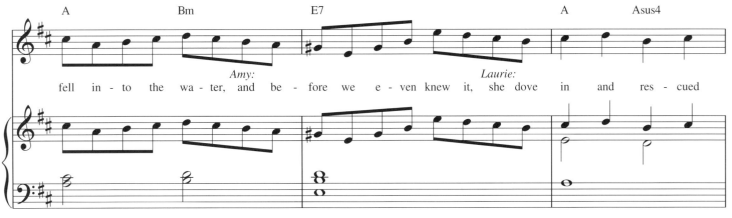

fell in-to the wa-ter, and be-fore we e-ven knew it, she dove in and res-cued

A little slower

me!

Amy: It hap-pened be-fore __ we knew.

Tempo I

Laurie: How could we have known? *Amy:* A-maz-ing what time __ can do. ___

Laurie: From that mo-ment my heart flew.

Amy: We'll be mar-ried in the

Days of Plenty

Lyrics by
Mindi Dickstein

Music by
Jason Howland

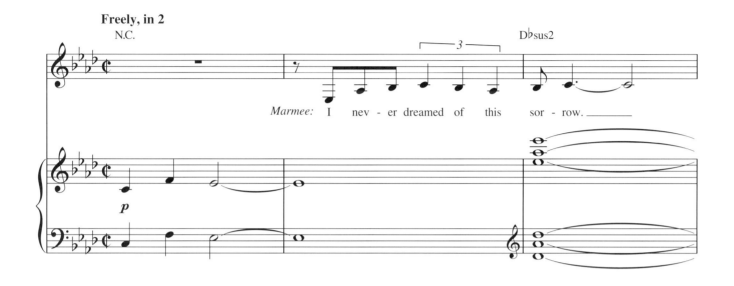

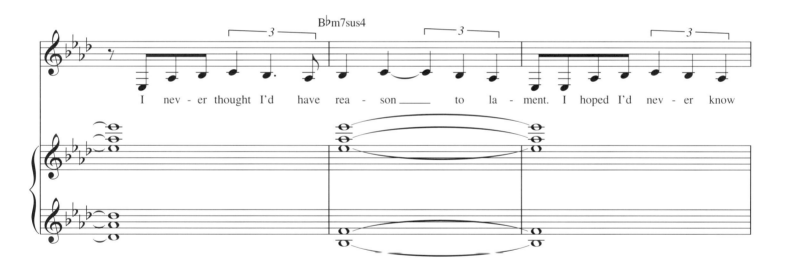

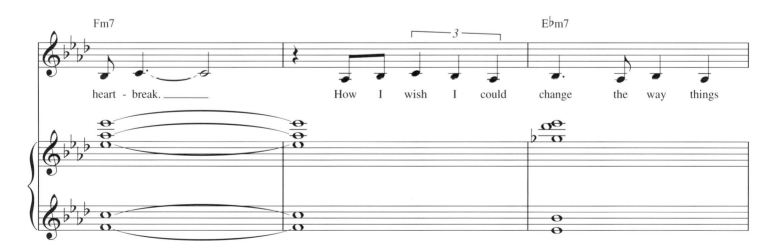

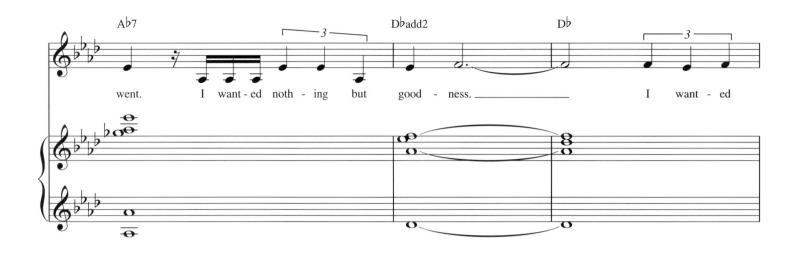

went. I want-ed noth - ing but good - ness. _____ I want - ed

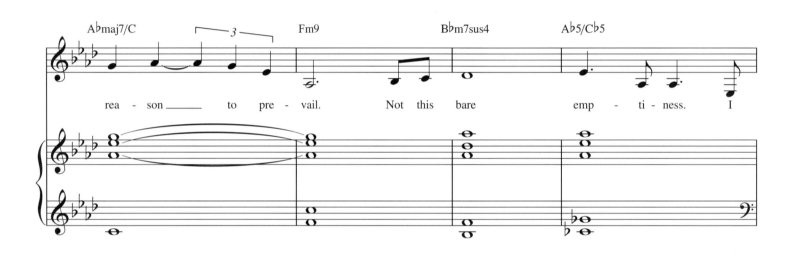

rea - son _____ to pre - vail. Not this bare emp - ti - ness. I

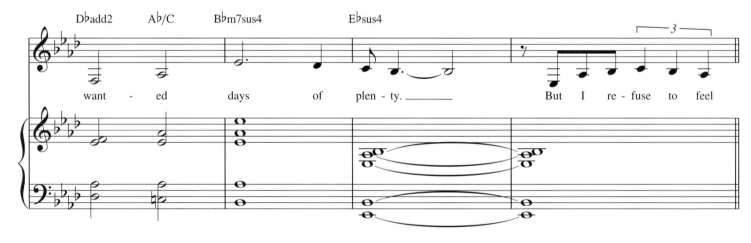

want - ed days of plen - ty. _____ But I re - fuse to feel

Moderately, in 2

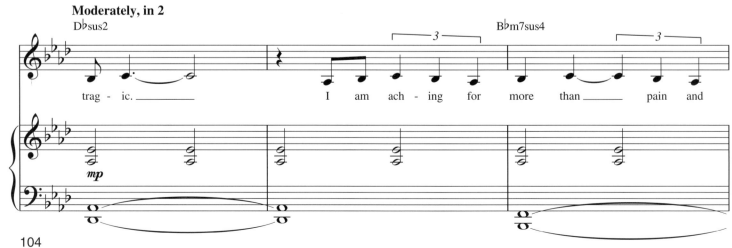

trag - ic. _____ I am ach - ing for more than _____ pain and

I want days of plen - ty. _____

You have _____ to be - lieve there is

rea - son _____ for hope. You have _____ to be -

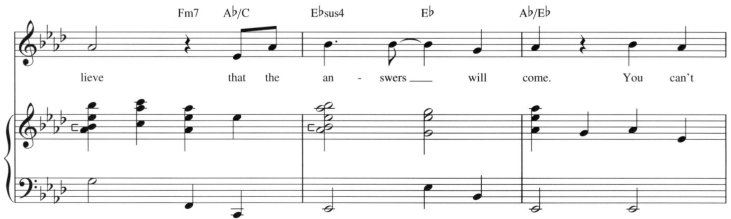

lieve that the an - swers _____ will come. You can't

The Fire Within Me

Lyrics by
Mindi Dickstein

Music by
Jason Howland

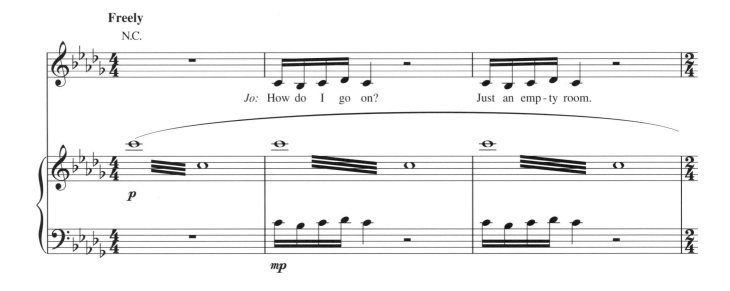

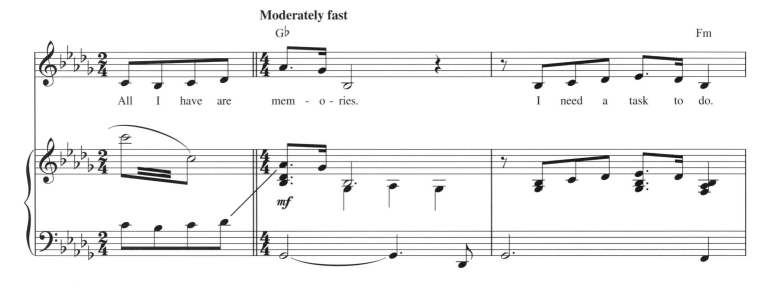

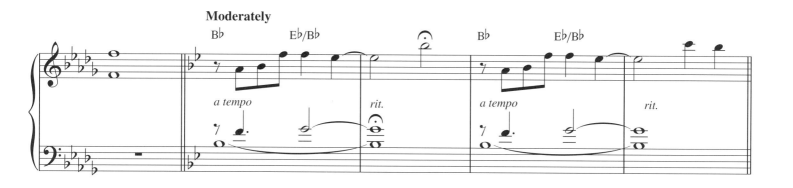

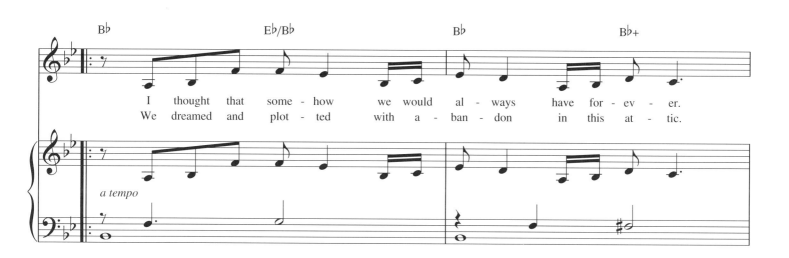

113

Small Umbrella in the Rain

Lyrics by
Mindi Dickstein

Music by
Jason Howland

Freely

P.B.: No. Yes! Yes! *I do not mean today, or tomorrow,*

or even next month, a year. Maybe two years, even. I'm a patient man.

Coda

there. Though we are

Slower (Moderately)

not at all a - like, you make me feel a -

More Great Piano/Vocal Books

FROM CHERRY LANE

For a complete listing of Cherry Lane titles available, including contents listings, please visit our web site at

www.cherrylane.com

02500343 Almost Famous $14.95
02502171 The Best of Boston $17.95
02500672 Black Eyed Peas – Elephunk . . . $17.95
02500665 Sammy Cahn Songbook $24.95
02500144 Mary Chapin Carpenter –
         Party Doll & Other Favorites . . $16.95
02502163 Mary Chapin Carpenter –
         Stones in the Road $17.95
02502165 John Denver Anthology –
         Revised $22.95
02502227 John Denver –
         A Celebration of Life. $14.95
02500002 John Denver Christmas $14.95
02502166 John Denver's Greatest Hits $17.95
02502151 John Denver – A Legacy
         in Song (Softcover) $24.95
02502152 John Denver – A Legacy
         in Song (Hardcover) $34.95
02500566 Poems, Prayers and Promises: The Art
         and Soul of John Denver $19.95
02500326 John Denver –
         The Wildlife Concert $17.95
02500501 John Denver and the Muppets:
         A Christmas Together $9.95
02509922 The Songs of Bob Dylan $29.95
02500586 Linda Eder – Broadway My Way $14.95
02500497 Linda Eder – Gold $14.95
02500396 Linda Eder –
         Christmas Stays the Same $17.95
02500175 Linda Eder –
         It's No Secret Anymore $14.95
02502209 Linda Eder – It's Time $17.95
02500630 Donald Fagen – 5 of the Best . . . $7.95
02500535 Erroll Garner Anthology $19.95
02500270 Gilbert & Sullivan for Easy Piano $12.95
02500318 Gladiator $12.95
02500273 Gold & Glory:
         The Road to El Dorado $16.95
02502126 Best of Guns N' Roses $17.95
02502072 Guns N' Roses – Selections from
         Use Your Illusion I and II $17.95
02500014 Sir Roland Hanna Collection . . . $19.95
02500352 Hanson – This Time Around . . . $16.95
02502134 Best of Lenny Kravitz $12.95
02500012 Lenny Kravitz – 5 . . . . $16.95
02500381 Lenny Kravitz – Greatest Hits . . . $14.95
02503701 Man of La Mancha $10.95

02500693 Dave Matthews – Some Devil . . . $16.95
02500555 Dave Matthews Band –
         Busted Stuff $16.95
02500003 Dave Matthews Band – Before
         These Crowded Streets $17.95
02502199 Dave Matthews Band – Crash . . $17.95
02500390 Dave Matthews Band –
         Everyday $14.95
02500493 Dave Matthews Band – Live in Chicago
         12/19/98 at the United Center . $14.95
02502192 Dave Matthews Band – Under
         the Table and Dreaming $17.95
02500681 John Mayer – Heavier Things . . $16.95
02500563 John Mayer – Room for Squares $16.95
02500081 Natalie Merchant – Ophelia $14.95
02500423 Natalie Merchant – Tigerlily . . . $14.95
02502895 Nine $17.95
02500425 Time and Love: The Art and
         Soul of Laura Nyro $19.95
02502204 The Best of Metallica $17.95
02500407 O-Town $14.95
02500010 Tom Paxton – The Honor
         of Your Company $17.95
02507962 Peter, Paul & Mary –
         Holiday Concert $17.95
02500145 Pokemon 2.B.A. Master $12.95
02500026 The Prince of Egypt $16.95
02500660 Best of Bonnie Raitt $17.95
02502189 The Bonnie Raitt Collection $22.95
02502230 Bonnie Raitt – Fundamental . . . $17.95
02502139 Bonnie Raitt –
         Longing in Their Hearts $16.95
02502088 Bonnie Raitt – Luck of the Draw $14.95
02507958 Bonnie Raitt – Nick of Time . . . $14.95
02502190 Bonnie Raitt – Road Tested $24.95
02502218 Kenny Rogers – The Gift $16.95
02500072 Saving Private Ryan $14.95
02500197 SHeDAISY –
         The Whole SHeBANG $14.95
02500414 Shrek $14.95
02500536 Spirit – Stallion of the Cimarron $16.95
02500166 Steely Dan – Anthology $17.95
02500622 Steely Dan –
         Everything Must Go $14.95
02500284 Steely Dan –
         Two Against Nature $14.95
02500165 Best of Steely Dan $14.95

02500344 Billy Strayhorn:
         An American Master. $17.95
02502132 Barbra Streisand –
         Back to Broadway $19.95
02500515 Barbra Streisand –
         Christmas Memories $16.95
02507969 Barbra Streisand – A Collection:
         Greatest Hits and More $17.95
02502164 Barbra Streisand – The Concert $22.95
02500550 Essential Barbra Streisand $24.95
02502228 Barbra Streisand –
         Higher Ground. $16.95
02500196 Barbra Streisand –
         A Love Like Ours $16.95
02500280 Barbra Streisand – Timeless . . . $19.95
02503617 John Tesh – Avalon $15.95
02502178 The John Tesh Collection $17.95
02503623 John Tesh – A Family Christmas $15.95
02505511 John Tesh –
         Favorites for Easy Piano $12.95
02503630 John Tesh – Grand Passion $16.95
02500124 John Tesh – One World $14.95
02500307 John Tesh – Pure Movies 2 . . . . $16.95
02500565 Thoroughly Modern Millie $17.95
02500576 Toto – 5 of the Best. $7.95
02502175 Tower of Power –
         Silver Anniversary $17.95
02502198 The "Weird Al" Yankovic
         Anthology. $17.95
02502217 Trisha Yearwood –
         A Collection of Hits $16.95
02500334 Maury Yeston – December Songs $17.95
02502225 The Maury Yeston Songbook . . . $19.95

See your local music dealer or contact:

CHERRY LANE
MUSIC COMPANY
6 East 32nd Street, New York, NY 10016
Quality in Printed Music

EXCLUSIVELY DISTRIBUTED BY

HAL•LEONARD®
CORPORATION
7777 W. BLUEMOUND RD. P.O. BOX 13819 MILWAUKEE, WI 53213

Prices, contents and availability subject to change without notice.

0404

More Big-Note & Easy Piano Books

For a complete listing of Cherry Lane titles available, including contents listings, please visit our web site at www.cherrylane.com

CLASSICAL CHRISTMAS
Easy solo arrangements of 30 wonderful holiday songs: Ave Maria • Dance of the Sugar Plum Fairy • Evening Prayer • Gesu Bambino • Hallelujah! • He Shall Feed His Flock • March of the Toys • O Come, All Ye Faithful • O Holy Night • Pastoral Symphony • Sheep May Safely Graze • Sinfonia • Waltz of the Flowers • and more.
__02500112 Easy Piano Solo $9.95

BEST OF JOHN DENVER
__02505512 Easy Piano $9.95

DOWN THE AISLE
Easy piano arrangements of 20 beloved pop and classical wedding songs, including: Air on the G String • Ave Maria • Canon in D • Follow Me • Give Me Forever (I Do) • Jesu, Joy of Man's Desiring • Prince of Denmark's March • Through the Years • Trumpet Tune • Unchained Melody • Wedding March • When I Fall in Love • You Decorated My Life • and more.
__025000267 Easy Piano $9.95

EASY BROADWAY SHOWSTOPPERS
Easy piano arrangements of 16 traditional and new Broadway standards, including: "Impossible Dream" from Man of La Mancha • "Unusual Way" from Nine • "This Is the Moment" from Jekyll & Hyde • many more.
__02505517 Easy Piano $12.95

GOLD AND GLORY – THE ROAD TO EL DORADO
This beautiful souvenir songbook features full-color photos and 8 songs from the DreamWorks animated film. Includes original songs by Elton John and Tim Rice, and a score by Hans Zimmer and John Powell. Songs: Cheldorado – Score • El Dorado • Friends Never Say Goodbye • It's Tough to Be a God • Someday out of the Blue (Theme from El Dorado) • The Trail We Blaze • Without Question • Wonders of the New World: To Shibalba.
__02500274 Easy Piano $14.95

A FAMILY CHRISTMAS AROUND THE PIANO
25 songs for hours of family fun, including: Away in a Manger • Deck the Hall • The First Noel • God Rest Ye Merry, Gentlemen • Hark! the Herald Angels Sing • Jingle Bells • Jolly Old St. Nicholas • Joy to the World • O Little Town of Bethlehem • Silent Night, Holy Night • The Twelve Days of Christmas • and more.
__02500398 Easy Piano $7.95

GILBERT & SULLIVAN FOR EASY PIANO
20 great songs from 6 great shows by this beloved duo renowned for their comedic classics. Includes: Behold the Lord High Executioner • The Flowers That Bloom in the Spring • He Is an Englishman • I Am the Captain of the Pinafore (I'm Called) Little Buttercup • Miya Sama • Three Little Maids • Tit-Willow • We Sail the Ocean Blue • When a Merry Maiden Marries • When Britain Really Ruled the Waves • When Frederic Was a Lad • and more.
__02500270 Easy Piano $12.95

GREAT CONTEMPORARY BALLADS
__02500150 Easy Piano $12.95

HOLY CHRISTMAS CAROLS COLORING BOOK
A terrific songbook with 7 sacred carols and lots of coloring pages for the young pianist. Songs include: Angels We Have Heard on High • The First Noel • Hark! The Herald Angels Sing • It Came upon a Midnight Clear • O Come All Ye Faithful • O Little Town of Bethlehem • Silent Night.
__02500277 Five-Finger Piano $6.95

JEKYLL & HYDE – VOCAL SELECTIONS
Ten songs from the Wildhorn/Bricusse Broadway smash, arranged for big-note: In His Eyes • It's a Dangerous Game • Lost in the Darkness • A New Life • No One Knows Who I Am • Once Upon a Dream • Someone Like You • Sympathy, Tenderness • Take Me as I Am • This Is the Moment.
__02505515 Easy Piano $12.95
__02500023 Big-Note Piano $9.95

JUST FOR KIDS – NOT! CHRISTMAS SONGS
This unique collection of 14 Christmas favorites is fun for the whole family! Kids can play the full-sounding big-note solos alone, or with their parents (or teachers) playing accompaniment for the thrill of four-hand piano! Includes: Deck the Halls • Jingle Bells • Silent Night • What Child Is This? • and more.
__02505510 Big-Note Piano $7.95

JUST FOR KIDS – NOT! CLASSICS
Features big-note arrangements of classical masterpieces, plus optional accompaniment for adults. Songs: Air on the G String • Dance of the Sugar Plum Fairy • Für Elise • Jesu, Joy of Man's Desiring • Ode to Joy • Pomp and Circumstance • The Sorcerer's Apprentice • William Tell Overture • and more!
__02505513 Classics....................$7.95
__02500301 More Classics $7.95

JUST FOR KIDS – NOT! FUN SONGS
Fun favorites for kids everywhere in big-note arrangements for piano, including: Bingo • Eensy Weensy Spider • Farmer in the Dell • Jingle Bells • London Bridge • Pop Goes the Weasel • Puff the Magic Dragon • Skip to My Lou • Twinkle, Twinkle Little Star • and more!
__02505523 Fun Songs................$7.95
__02505528 More Fun Songs $7.95

JUST FOR KIDS – NOT! TV THEMES & MOVIE SONGS
Entice the kids to the piano with this delightful collection of songs and themes from movies and TV. These big-note arrangements include themes from The Brady Bunch and The Addams Family, as well as Do-Re-Mi (The Sound of Music), theme from Beetlejuice (Day-O) and Puff the Magic Dragon. Each song includes an accompaniment part for teacher or adult so that the kids can experience the joy of four-hand playing as well! Plus performance tips.
__02505507 TV Themes & Movie Songs $9.95
__02500304 More TV Themes & Movie Songs $9.95

LOVE BALLADS
__02500152 EZ-Play Today #364 $7.95

MERRY CHRISTMAS, EVERYONE
Over 20 contemporary and classic all-time holiday favorites arranged for big-note piano or easy piano. Includes: Away in a Manger • Christmas Like a Lullaby • The First Noel • Joy to the World • The Marvelous Toy • and more.
__02505600 Big-Note Piano $9.95

POKEMON 2 B.A. MASTER
This great songbook features easy piano arrangements of 13 tunes from the hit TV series: 2.B.A. Master • Double Trouble (Team Rocket) • Everything Changes • Misty's Song • My Best Friends • Pokémon (Dance Mix) • Pokémon Theme • PokéRAP • The Time Has Come (Pikachu's Goodbye) • Together, Forever • Viridian City • What Kind of Pokémon Are You? • You Can Do It (If You Really Try). Includes a full-color, 8-page pull-out section featuring characters and scenes from this super hot show.
__02500145 Easy Piano $12.95

POKEMON
Five-finger arrangements of 7 songs from the hottest show for kids! Includes: Pokémon Theme • The Time Has Come (Pikachu's Goodbye) • 2B A Master • Together, Forever • What Kind of Pokémon Are You? • You Can Do It (If You Really Try). Also features cool character artwork, and a special section listing the complete lyrics for the "PokéRAP."
__02500291 Five-Finger Piano $7.95

POP/ROCK HITS
__02500153 E-Z Play Today #366 $7.95

POP/ROCK LOVE SONGS
Easy arrangements of 18 romatic favorites, including: Always • Bed of Roses • Butterfly Kisses • Follow Me • From This Moment On • Hard Habit to Break • Leaving on a Jet Plane • When You Say Nothing at All • more.
__02500151 Easy Piano $10.95

POPULAR CHRISTMAS CAROLS COLORING BOOK
Kids are sure to love this fun holiday songbook! It features five-finger piano arrangements of seven Christmas classics, complete with coloring pages throughout! Songs include: Deck the Hall • Good King Wenceslas • Jingle Bells • Jolly Old St. Nicholas • O Christmas Tree • Up on the Housetop • We Wish You a Merry Christmas.
__02500276 Five-Finger Piano $6.95

PUFF THE MAGIC DRAGON & 54 OTHER ALL-TIME CHILDREN'S FAVORITE SONGS
55 timeless songs enjoyed by generations of kids, and sure to be favorites for years to come. Songs include: A-Tisket A-Tasket • Alouette • Eensy Weensy Spider • The Farmer in the Dell • I've Been Working on the Railroad • If You're Happy and You Know It • Joy to the World • Michael Finnegan • Oh Where, Oh Where Has My Little Dog Gone • Silent Night • Skip to My Lou • This Old Man • and many more.
__02500017 Big-Note Piano $12.95

PURE ROMANCE
__02500268 Easy Piano $10.95

SCHOOLHOUSE ROCK SONGBOOK
10 unforgettable songs from the classic television educational series, now experiencing a booming resurgence in popularity from Generation X'ers to today's kids! Includes: I'm Just a Bill • Conjunction Junction • Lolly, Lolly, Lolly (Get Your Adverbs Here) • The Great American Melting Pot • and more.
__02505576 Big-Note Piano $8.95

BEST OF JOHN TESH
__02505511 Easy Piano $12.95
__02500128 E-Z Play Today #356 $8.95

TOP COUNTRY HITS
__02500154 E-Z Play Today #365 $7.95

Prices, contents, and availability subject to change without notice.

1001